North Country
Biographies - 1

Great Uncle Ned's trip
to Hamburg

Moira Rutherford

White & Co.
7 Front Street
Lanchester
Durham DH7 0LA

SOURCES

The photographs and original information came from Mrs Mary Wilkinson and she and her brothers, Uncle Arthur and Uncle Wilf Rutherford and other members of the family helped tremendously by talking about their recollections of Ned Kay and reading what I had assembled.

The news of the men and conditions in the Consett area during the first world war came from newspapers in Newcastle Central Library, Durham County Library and the British Library. *The Consett Guardian, Durham County Advertiser, The Journal*, and the *Newcastle Evening Chronicle*.

I learned about life in Ruhleben by reading:

Brown, Percy, *Round the Corner*, 1934, Faber

Cohen, Israel, *The Ruhleben Prison Camp*, 1917, Methuen

Gerard, James W, *My Four Years in Germany*, 1917, Hodder & Stoughton

Ketchum J Davidson, *A Prison Camp Society*, 1965, Toronto and OUP

Mahoney, Henry C, *Interned in Germany*, 1918, Sampson Low, Marston & Co., Ltd

Powell J & Gribble Francis H, *History of Ruhleben*, 1919

Pyke, E.L, *Desperate in Germany*, 1918, Hodder & Stoughton

Pyke, G.N, *To Ruhleben — and back;* a great adventure in three phases, 1916, Constable & Co

ISBN 0 9519410 0 3

British Library Cataloguing - in Publication Data
A catalogue record for this book is available from
the British Library

Typeset in ITC Bookman in Postscript using PageMaker 4 by Smithfield Publishing Ltd., High Street, Castle Camps, Cambs CB1 6SN and printed by Rivermead Design, Unit 4A Baddow Park, West Hanningfield Road, Great Baddow, Chelmsford, Essex CM2 7SY

Delayed by the Kaiser

I may never have met my dad's Uncle Ned. But my cousin Betty, who is only a year older, certainly did because she remembers his nose, bulbous, cratered and red. Great Uncle Ned only intruded on my consciousness after he died. And that was because he didn't leave a will. My father had to sort out the estate and, as a result, some kids down the street called Telford told me they were relations.

Thirty years later Auntie Mary gave me some photographs,including some first world war pictures of a Norman Telford in the Durham Light Infantry and an old postcard of Watling Street addressed in 1915 to Ned at Ruhleben Spandau which I vaguely recognised as the name of an underground station in Berlin. What was he doing there?

'Oh, He went to Hamburg on his holidays and spent the next four years stuck in Germany,' said Auntie Mary.

Holidays abroad and Hamburg of all places!

George Edward (Ned) Kay was brother to Lily Rutherford, my grandmother and so my father's and Auntie Mary's uncle. (Telfords, it turned out, were grandchildren of Granny's elder sister.) At the age of 37 he was working on the screen at Medomsley Colliery and living with his widowed mother, Mrs Bessie Kay, at Derwent Cottages.

He had possibly been abroad before the disastrous German trip. There is a photograph, a Carte-Postale, Ned, plump, shiny and dapper in his best black suit with a Kaiser-style moustache waxed jauntily. The studio background gives the appearance of a very grandly draped window of a continental type. With him, on that occasion, was his uncle Joseph Whittaker, looking very sprightly although he must have been nearly 70 years old,

A pre-war studio picture of Ned (centre) with his Uncle Joe Whittaker (left) and GeorgeRichardson

and his gaffer at work, George Richardson. They were all bachelors, and may have gone no further than Whitley Bay...but the picture has an out and 'abroad' feel that could mean a weekend in Ostend.

Miners did not get paid holidays in 1914 but Ned hadn't a family to keep and it can't have been too difficult for George, who was the older man, to tempt Ned and another mate,Tom Parker, to join him on his annual trip to sample the delights of the Reeperbahn in Hamburg over the August bank holiday. More surprisingly, there was a fourth member of the party, Mr G Holliday of Allendale Cottages, older than them all, and married.

Perhaps they read in the papers about the assassination in the Balkans. But how could four miners intent on pleasure work out the international situation when their political leaders didn't know what was about to happen?

It is possible that George had connections that got them a cheap passage on one of the Tyne merchant boats carrying coal to Germany. There was, of course, a regular passenger service: the Tyne-Tees Shipping Company advertised regular sailings direct to the Continent from Newcastle. Fares to Hamburg were 30 shillings and 16s.6d single and 35 shillings and 26s.6d. for a three month return.

It was a sun-filled summer and the steamships were packed with the English heading for Germany, schoolmasters and academics going on courses, professional men and students to walk in the Black Forest, whole families for cultural trips to Berlin. Troubles in the Balkans were endemic and no matter of concern to the English travelling in Northern Europe.

The *New Londoner* left for Hamburg on Saturdays, returning Tuesday night and the men could have taken it on July 25. It left the Tyne again on August 1, weighing anchor at 9 am unaware that Germany was already delaying ships from leaving its harbours.

They might have just made it home if *The New Londoner* had been able to leave on schedule the following Tuesday morning. Britain declared war on Germany on Tuesday, August 4. Germany, already in a state of mobilization, detained all British ships in its harbours promptly. Long afterwards the families of the Durham men heard that the holidaymakers had already been on board for the journey home when the police came to take them and the sailors off to prison. Ned was not to see home again for three and a half years.

War 1914-1915

In England, the news that came through was not hopeful. On August 5, *The Journal* published a statement from the manager of a shipping line that a message had been received from Hamburg announcing that the Germans were detaining the steamship *Leversons*, which had just completed discharging a cargo of coal. And within an hour there had been news that an oil ship was also being held and it was hinted that possibly the Germans would close down on 40 other steamers.

In Consett, the territorials were recalled from camp, reassembled, marched off to the railway station headed by the Consett Military Band and entrained for headquarters at Bishop Auckland.

Schools were reopened so the children could be fed, removing a big expense from parents whose breadwinners were thrown out of work.

John Wilson, the Durham Miners' leader, thanked coal owners for allowing families of Reservists to remain in colliery houses and giving them coal. The widow Mrs Kay must have been desperately worried about the roof over her head with one miner son missing and her younger sons liable to march off to war.

In spite of the war news and rumours flooding in, the *Consett Guardian* gave space to express anxiety about the missing holiday men.

Britain too was mopping up the foreigners on her territory. Five German reservists, who had been constructing new patent Otto coke ovens for the Consett Iron Company, were arrested at Langley Park.

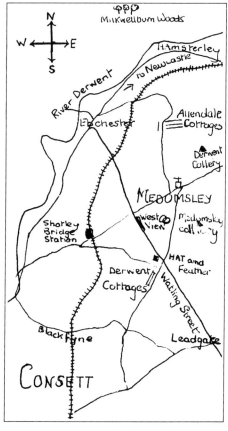

Some news of missing Britons filtered through, John Armstrong, son of the Consett postmaster, third engineer in the *San Wilfredo* when it sunk, was safe in Hamburg, reported the *Consett Guardian*. But it was a month before the first news of the Medomsley miners came in the form of a letter to Mrs Holliday. They were all right but in confinement.

Then in September, Mr Holliday came home after six weeks as a prisoner of war. He was the only member of the party above fighting age - the others had had to stay.

In November, another returning Englishman, Dr J.J. Paterson, from Maidenhead, who had been arrested in Hamburg on August 4, brought news that when he had left a concentration camp in Hanover, Thomas Parker, of 102 Allendale Cottages, Hamsterley Colliery, George Richardson of 18 West View, Medomsley and G.E. Kay of 2 Derwent Cottages, Medomsley were in good health.

Ned and his mates didn't speak German - they were all elementary schoolboys who had been doing long hours at manual work since they were 12 or 14. But they had obviously fallen in with people who could.

Probably it was very frightening but as the over-45s got away it may have seemed only a temporary embarrassment. Later they would realise their treatment was less harsh than that of the seamen who were kept for months in miserable conditions on abandoned hulks in Hamburg harbour.

It is unlikely that any of them had any money left and they had no means at all to find out what was happening in Britain and no contact with home. Food in German prisons ranged from the non-existent to the sparse and without money to supplement the prison fare which could be as little as one meal a day of bread and water, Ned must have lost weight rapidly.

Then in the late afternoon twilight of November 6, 1914 Ned was among about 4,000 civilians of military age, who were marched into an improvised camp at Ruhleben racecourse in a Berlin suburb, a mile east of Spandau. It was a raw misty day with heavy grey clouds.

Their billets were stables and lofts. Men were housed six to a horse-box 11 feet square or toe-to-toe in the lofts above.

Ned must have been one of earlier arrivals because he was in barrack 3, one of the permanent brick built stables on the perimeter on the side of the main gates next to the road and railway - wooden barracks were built to house late-comers.

The prisoners were shoved by guards into billets in the order in which they filed in. As Ned and the other pitmen would stick together they must have been billeted near each other. There was no attempt to segregate men by age, class or occupation. All were tumbled together in cramped conditions, peer and circus clown, sailor and business man, schoolmaster and engineer.

It was typical November weather, rainy and cold. Some men who had come straight from homes in Germany were winter-clad and had packed a few comforts in their suitcases. Ned and his mates had only their midsummer holiday clothes.

There was a thin layer of straw on the cement floors for sleeping but manure from previous inhabitants during the trotting races was still lying around. Early arrivals got one blanket, later the supply ran out. There was no heating. Some men got thin cocoa and blood sausage to eat, some got nothing that day.

Israel Cohen, a journalist who had been caught in Berlin and was in the camp for 19 months before being exchanged on health grounds, said that many groups of prisoners, some in light summer clothes, were kept standing about for hours before they were assigned to billets in the stables. Many were drenched by the rain.

Joseph Powell and Francis Gribble, who wrote a *History of Ruhleben, a record of British organisation in a prison camp in Germany*, said that the racecourse surface was dry, loose, dirty sand. Rain transformed it into mud that autumn so the men had to wade a quarter of a mile three times a day to collect food from the kitchens which were underneath the Grandstand or just to visit the revolting latrines. 'Men without money were left to wash without soap, eat with their fingers and drink by putting their mouths to the tap,' wrote Powell and Gribble.

There were no letters from home, no means of writing home. Appel was at 7 o clock. Unlike 'other rank' first world war prisoners, the internees were not compelled to work. So the miners at least had a break from the hard labour in the pits where they earned their peace-time living. On the other hand they had little opportunity to earn money.

Money would have helped in the first hungry months but they must have been used to dirt, damp and discomfort for long hours at work. But here there was no daily escape to coal fires and home baking.

Percy Brown, a news man, who wrote about his time in Ruhleben in his book, *Round the Corner*, says that some people earned money from working for other prisoners - he had a circus performer for a servant who washed his pots, made his bed, cooked meals.

Officers in those class conscious days were treated very differently in first-world-war Germany. They were kept in separate camps from the men and were usually able to have a fair life style with lavish food parcels from home. But conditions in military prisoner-of-war camps were poor for ordinary soldiers and many didn't survive the combination of hard labour, malnutrition and brutal treatment.

As the war went on, there was stringent rationing for the German civil population, and a near-starvation diet for alien prisoners was not considered unreasonable under the circumstances.

Black bread, watery soup and ersatz coffee was the order of the day. So the Durham pitmen were lucky to be in a civilian internment camp where men were offered no special treatment for social status.

At Ruhleben some German women had a concessionary canteen where those with funds could supplement their rations with rolls and butter. But nearly half the camp, 2,000 men, were destitute and that must have included Ned and his mates.

When the American Ambassador came to visit the camp in late November or early December, a man from the crowd shouted 'We're starving here, Sir. For God's sake send us some bread,' and Gribble,

Ned is fourth from the left, George Richardson, probably far left

10

who reported this said: 'the men, who, unassisted from an outside source had to live on their rations, got up hungry in the morning and went to bed hungry at night.'

Winter was grim but the interpreters from each barracks had formed themselves into a Captains' Committee and were beginning to organise improvements. The American Ambassador wrote afterwards that he had 'found it quite impossible to get British prisoners to perform the ordinary work of cleaning up the camp...always expected of prisoners themselves'. So he handed over British Government money so the camp captain Powell could pay poorer prisoners to do the work. An occasional grant of five marks was made to the penniless from a charitable fund, money was raised to get the latrines cleaned, and a voluntary civilian police force was started. Some heating was installed.

The first winter was the hardest time of the four years in the camp: the racecourse, built on reclaimed marshland was damp, dreary, windswept and cold.

A photograph of Ned and his marras must have been taken that winter because there is a German guard and they were to disappear from inside the camp within the year. There is snow lying on the ground and the men are standing outside the glass doors of a building.There is a large printed label on the door but only a few letters are visible. The windows on either side are so large it might almost be a conservatory or a summer teahouse - perhaps that was what it was. The building is of light brick with darker bricks used in a geometrical pattern.

Ned looks thin and frail and wears a cap and waistcoat and may be wearing clogs. On Auntie Mary's copy there are red ink crosses on two other men in the group. One is probably George Richardson and he has a skimpy cardigan buttoned at the top but not stretching over his chest. The other is a younger man, clean shaven and wearing a ribbed sweater. Another man is in shirt sleeves and the one man with a jacket of sorts has a peaked cap and the look of a sailor. There isn't a collar or tie among them. They all look like working men.

Percy Brown said that although there was some mixing in the camp, class distinctions were sharply defined. He was perhaps a more objective observer of this particular aspect than many as he didn't belong to either the public school or business communities, was middle class by virtue of his job but had started his career as a workman. He only arrived at Ruhleben in 1915 after being tricked over the border when covering the war as a reporter and he spent months in ordinary prisons on suspicion of spying.

J. Davidson Ketchum in *Ruhleben: A Prison camp society* published in 1965 said that prisoners were as unequal as they well could be in birth, education, and social position but this was not at first noticeable. Once settled old class conventions were re-established.

But Ketchum, who had been a young piano student in Berlin before internment in Ruhleben, and only later a social psychologist maintained it was not a class ridden society because men learned to appreciate the outlook of others while living in such close quarters for so long.

Seamen monopolised the camp's manual work but as Ketchum groups factory workers and stable hands with the seamen it does not preclude the possibility that Ned found a job.

Although the first months were cold and hungry conditions started to improve. Some British parcels containing a few luxuries had arrived in December, 1914. In January 8,000 parcels came and, by June, the monthly total had risen to 27,000.

Charitable organisations raised parcel funds, so prisoners whose families could not supply them were not forgotten.

In March 1915 the men were able to send letters for the first time and Mrs Kay got news direct from her son after nine months' silence. Ned must have sent a postcard to friends as well because there is an answer surviving, written on a picture postcard of Watling Street, Leadgate and addressed to G. E. Kay, Kriegskamper, Englanderlager, Ruhleben. Spandau, Germany, from the Milburn family .

'Dear friend,' it says, 'received Post card glad to hear from you we are sending two Parcels with all you asked for it write back.'

In April of 1915, dole at the rate of five marks a week was given to the poorer prisoners by the British Government. It was intended as a loan but no attempt was made to collect after the war. Later when the supply of food parcels improved, this

Summer in Ruhleben

allowance was reduced to four marks.

In June summer outfits, light shirts, trousers, underwear, socks and shoes were provided for a nominal price of one mark.

Auntie Mary's second photograph of the unfortunate miner holidaymakers was a summer one, three men against a natural background of trees — the sun seems to glint through the birch leaves. It was probably the patch of woodlands to the east of the Tea House which Ketchum says was the only decent view in an area of smoking chimneys.George and Tom are hatless and sit on chairs placed on sandy ground. Ned, wearing a flat cap, is standing behind. All the men are casually dressed in trousers, waistcoats and rolled-up shirt sleeves. Ned's watch chain is in evidence and they seem to be wearing square blocked boots with heavy soles that are probably the clogs Percy Brown says were worn by many of the men. These were woodensoled, made in Germany and obtained through the canteen.

The men look strained. Ned, in particular, looks 'stretched on a rack of hope', the phrase used by H.C. Mahoney in *Interned in Germany* of men who had applied for repatriation. He described how when their names were called out at rollcall to have their photographs taken, there was a mad rush to the corner of the camp where the man with the camera had pitched his studio consisting of a bench capable of receiving three sitters at one time. This officially sponsored photograph cost each of the men 1s. 6d.

Eric Blumer of Darlington, a 20-year-old student when war broke out, had a box camera in Ruhleben. He told his family the Germans suspected he had it and once ripped the barracks apart looking for it, although it was in plain view all the time sitting on a tin of Rowntrees cocoa. He took pictures secretly including one of a Zeppelin flying over the race course.

Despair at home

If conditions were getting better in Ruhleben the news from home was fearful. Durham newspapers in 1915 had columns and columns devoted to the war dead and wounded, letters from soldiers at the front about 'the hell let loose', editorials on 'families with 6 or 7 sons who don't know where their duty lies'.

In some ways the world war might have been a better time for miners' families - the demand for coal become so great that there was work for all. But hours were long in the mines and the pressures to win more and more coal were heavy. And sons, uncles, fathers and brothers were volunteering for the front.

In 1916 Ned heard that his youngest brother, 23-year-old Wilf, had been killed in France on the first day of the Somme offensive. Wilf was a miner and need not have gone. The family story is that he enlisted in the Tyneside Scottish after an episode in a bus when he was mocked by the brother of a friend. The brother became a conscientious objector and survived the war, but his friend joined up as well and died. Later one of her neighbours came home on leave and told Mrs Kay he had been in the trenches when Wilf was blown to pieces next to him.

Then Ned's sprightly 70-year-old Uncle Joe Whittaker, who had lived with them, walked out of the stone house at Derwent Cottages and was never seen again.

Mrs Bessie Kay was getting old herself. All Ned's brothers were

Wilf Kay who died on the Somme

miners, except Alf who had a barber's shop at Number One until constant pain caused him to give up. Jack, the eldest, was already over 40 when war broke out, Arthur, a shot-putter, had contracted a wasting miners' disease that would kill him in seven years and Tom, the natty dresser, went off to the munitions' factory in Dunston but in October 1915 he died in Newcastle's Royal Victoria Hospital with a ruptured duodenal ulcer. Ned was far away and her oldest grandson, Norman Telford, who had lived with her since the death of her older daughter, had joined the Durham Light Infantry.

Fortunately the sons of her younger daughter, Lily Rutherford, my grandmother, were far too young to go to war. After a baby boy was born to Lily at Allendale Cottages in March, 1915 Ned learned that he had been called Wilfred after the young brother.

It was a long way from Berlin. Food parcels at Ruhleben could mean the difference between moderately adequate eating and malnutrition. Ned's family was poor. Moreover the cost of food was rising in England and this hit hardest at the working classes because this was a war when only the well off could buy what they wanted.

The newsman, Percy Brown reported that after a period of anarchy in the internment camp a central parcels committee was formed and every man got his share. Ketchum said that after December 16, 1915, every man was provided with three Red Cross parcels a fortnight and personal parcels were restricted to four a year.

Everything was in tins - the men relied on the parcels for their food for the rest of the war. Regular despatches of bread were started from Denmark and Sweden. A typical parcel might contain tinned steak and onions, corned beef, baked beans, cocoa, milk, sugar, tinned herrings, soap, soup, cigarettes and tobacco.*

In a short time, the camp was alive with activities, clubs, language classes, debates, concerts, plays. Magazines were printed and published.

There are copious records of these activities. Ketchum was able to consult 379 letters and postcards and ten diaries in the Ruhleben collection at Harvard. But he says the information and comments he collected came almost entirely from middle class people.

Only 16.5 per cent of the prisoners were workmen and their voice only comes through the veil of middle class attitudes. Uncle Ned's nephews say he was a very sociable man, so he may well have enjoyed the company after the first frightening months were over.

1917

Life went on steadily at Ruhleben. In January, 1917, the Allies and the Axis agreed to exchange prisoners of military age. But nothing happened at Ruhleben. There was little good news from the war but food parcels continued to arrive, except for a period in 1917 when the naval blockade took a grip.

It was the one serious shortage of food noticed by Percy Brown, who had money enough not to have been too much inconvenienced by earlier scarcities. There was even a blip in bread supplies which came from abroad.

The British government had organised bakeries to supply the prison camps - they had no faith in German black bread either.

Winter, 1917, was bitter in England too as German U-boats took a heavy toll of British merchant shipping. Lloyd George set up a Food Ministry to encourage voluntary rationing. It didn't result in anything like fair shares. The ordinary housewife had to spend much time in food queues.

Then, on Christmas Eve, 1917, 350 Ruhlebeners were told they would be leaving Germany in January. Ned and George were among them.

The *Newcastle Evening Chronicle* reported that the Queen of The Netherlands had inspected ships and dockside premises in Amsterdam that it was believed were to be used for the repatriation of British and German troops.

A telegram to Medomsley on January 9, 1918 said Ned Kay and

This was the actual contents of a parcel sent to D.L.I. prisoners from a special fund for the purpose in November, 1917.

Left: Ned's brother Tom, natty in white stock with friends on a balmy pre-war day at the Hat and Feather

Below: Ned's nephew, Norman Telford at a D.L.I. camp at Blackhill

Far left: Ned's sprightly Uncle Joe Whittaker. In the black days of the war he walked out of the house at Derwent Cottages without his pension book and was never seen again

George Richardson had landed in England and would be home the following day.

The disembarkation took place in Boston Lincolnshire. There were 370 civilians among the 632 men repatriated. The vessels arrived on Saturday afternoon of January 5 but Home Office officials only arrived on Sunday evening and were taken out by tender to Boston Deeps where the vessels lay. Next morning the unloading started. Batches of men were transported to the Seamen's Institute. They walked down to the dock gates in the intense cold, carrying their luggage. One of the men told the Press Association that, although the ships were comfortable, the men had been aboard too long, in most cases since the previous Wednesday, and there had been some shortage of rations. Some of the returning seamen had spent time in Sennelager, an internment camp where conditions seemed to have been much worse than in Ruhleben.

The Durham men returned to Arctic-like blizzards and food shortages. Ned was so pale and thin his mother would not have recognised him but for his moustache.

The moustache even from this distance of years looks a fine specimen, with an upward spike at each side. Before the war it was in proportion but in prison it dominated his thin face

Auntie Mary, who was about 15 years old at the time, remembered the homecoming, particularly his nose, which hadn't lost its size or texture.

Changed world

The war still had a terrible 10 months to run. Nobody remembers Ned going on about his privations in Berlin. Life was too grim at home. Former neighbours and workmates were still dying in France every week. Perhaps the two returning miners were secretly relieved that they had been detained long enough to be almost over military age as British Army recruiters tried to claw in 50,000 more men from the mines. The resultant shortage of labour must have ensured that Ned got his job back.

On February 8 the *Consett Guardian* commented on the case of a 41-year-old Leadgate man with four children already doing a useful job as colliery mason and church sexton who had to go into the army at the end of the month leaving an old vicar to dig the graves 'with tens of thousands of strong and able young men available'. Just where these hordes were skulking in the fourth year of the war it did not say!

Basic foods were price-controlled - a grocer was reported for selling butter at 2s 5d a pound instead of 2s 4d and selling two pound loaves of bread for 5d instead of 4d.

Not surprisingly, Consett Iron and Steel workers held an Open Air meeting one Sunday calling for rationing because 'the unequal distribution of food' was 'unfair to the working classes whose labour

Above:
Great Grandmother Kay (1851-1927) in her back yard at Derwent Cottages, wearing what Uncle Arthur, called her 'washing-day blouse'.
She told her grandchildren that she walked to Lanchester to be wed and returned to serve in the bar of the Hat and Feather that evening. She had eight children who survived to become adults. Derwent Cottages are long gone but the Hat and Feather is still there

Top right: Grandmother Rutherford (1879-1931) at West View, Medomsley Edge. It was the last of the 18 houses she lived in after her marriage in 1900. Ned lived there too at the time of her death. Afterwards her daughter, Mary, with miner husband Billy Wilkinson, took over the house living there until his retirement

Right: Auntie Mary (1902-1992) in Milkwell Burn Woods. Mary was 12 years old when Ned went on his German holiday

called for a great expenditure of energy and which could only be restored by adequate food'.

Food rationing finally came towards the end of February. But there were still problems. One of the members of Lanchester Food Control Committee commented that 'whilst there was a shortage of jam, cheese and matches at the Co-operative Stores, private traders could get a good supply of these articles.'

In spite of union and Co-op protests only two boxes of matches a fortnight were supplied — no use to the miner who could get through a dozen boxes!

Government propaganda used the example of Ruhleben to persuade its citizens that the value of a well organised and well administered rationing system was that there was food enough for all if evenly shared.

The War Supplement for April 13, 1918 had a cartoon of two men in a railway compartment. One is a cigar-puffing Stout Party in top hat, fur collar and cuffed overcoat, and spats; the other a shabby cloth capped man with a wasted frame. Stout Party complains that ration cards are a 'dashed nuisance', Thin Party, who has just left Ruhleben, puts him to shame by reminding Stout Party that ration books were not needed to share out fairly there.

As Ned settled into war-time England, the remaining prisoners at Ruhleben were keeping occupied and reasonably fed because of the parcels from home - and their own gardening efforts. Ernest Pyke, repatriated in March 1918, said that the Germans, even in 1917, had feared that envious and starving Berliners would break into Ruhleben. As inspector of the camp kitchens he had been able to visit Berlin on licence.

Germans were suffering badly because of the British Blockade. The food situation was so grim that dogs and cats were being eaten in Berlin. On January 28, 1918 German workers went on strike. In Berlin feelings ran high and although workers were forced back within a week, revolution was in the air.

As the war ground to a halt there were new dangers. One sunny day the remaining internees heard a tremendous explosion, the huge grandstand was lifted as if by an earthquake. From the munition factories there was a tremendous grey wall of smoke, six miles long and the prisoners heard one explosion after another. Was it workers revolting or communists taking over?

Although strictly no longer prisoners, the Ruhlebeners were glad to have the guards to keep trouble out. Anarchy was all about and many Germans were starving. The internees knew about the October revolutions and the Kiel mutiny. Revolution was within daily sight - the railway line ran by the camp and one day the Ruhleben men saw a goods train go slowly past, stuck all over with red flags, loaded with sailors wielding machine guns.

The prison guards formed a soldiers' soviet and got themselves a red flag too - it was made in the prisoners' work shops. Officers remained in a group but were told to remove their badges and epaulettes and were spat upon by their men.

Late in November, 1918 the remaining Ruhleben prisoners set out for home. Perhaps this included the fourth miner, Tom Parker. They travelled in relative comfort in two trains to Denmark and sailed on the *Frecaria* to Leith. The Danes put themselves out to provision the boat well.

The *Durham County Advertiser* (December 5, 1918) reported the return of Mr Albert Henderson, nine years a clerk to a German merchant, now in a bad state of health after internment but making the point that 'Tommy had suffered more than they at Ruhleben'. And as the military prisoners of war returned with horrific tales of privation it was clear that the civilians had been fortunate. Some told of barbarities at the hands of the Turks, working barefoot in the mines, being knocked about by guards.

A Ferryhill man talked about the food; one slice of bread, weak barley coffee, mangolds, sour cabbage, potato peelings; working on a shell dump in all weathers where in nine weeks there had been 100 deaths from starvation and dysentery.

The *Consett Guardian* (December 13, 1918) said that all of the returning local prisoners of war complained of bad treatment and the food, 'two bowls of dirty soup, and on Sunday a little barley'. But there was danger at home too. Dr Buckham reporting to Lanchester Rural District Council at the end of 1918 said that influenza had been rampant in the district — 101 deaths in the month. At the workhouse infirmary matters were desperate with 29 deaths in a month.

But Ned survived that too. After the war, as cheap coal poured into Britain as a result of the reparations demanded by the Treaty of Versailles, the coal industry moved into recession. As wages were forced down there were strikes and lock-outs and close-downs. Ned spent most of the twenties and thirties on the dole. His nephew, Wilf, remembers that he got odd jobs at the Iron works and in the winter there was often snow shovelling for the council.

He never married. He lived at Derwent Cottages with his mother when he first came home. Then his eldest brother Jack married a widow and turned both Ned and Arthur, together with the old lady, out of their home. Ned didn't speak to Jack again.

Both Great Grandmother and Arthur then lived at West View. For reasons probably embedded in the 'means test' economy of the twenties and thirties, Ned moved about, living variously in lodgings at Consett, Cutlers Hall and a hostel near the Iron Works. He was also staying at West View, Medomsley Edge with his sister, Lily Rutherford, when she died on November 16, 1931. He moved on then. Young Wilf often visited him. 'He got his mail at West View and as a lad I was sent

1918 - General View - East End.   2342

Photographed in its final year as an internment camp, Ruhleben reverted to horse and motor racing after the war. Then in 1958 it was torn down to provide space for a new Berlin sewage plant

In the photograph left (taken in January, 1992 by Ramsey Rutherford) Susan Lasche is walking along the road which used to border the internment camp.
The area is even more industrial than in 1918 - the building and chimney could well have been there in Ned's time

Susan and Ramsey discovered and photographed the Klärwerk Ruhleben (purification) plant which they think is built on the old racecourse.
A map of the area shows Spandau, where Hesse was imprisoned, after another war, not much more than a mile north-west of the camp site on the other side of the River Spree

on my bike to deliver it. That's how I know he belonged to the Druids — they used to write to him.'

Ned was not a great drinking man in spite of his beery nose. It was the result, he told young Wilf, of scratching a spot. It finally got so bad that Dr Lyon took pity on him and organised an operation. So in his declining years Ned's nose was perfectly ordinary.

He lived to see another generation go off to war with Germany. He had a steady job working as a council labourer on the roads in the Second World War and came round to see his nephew in uniform when the newly married Wilf went into the army in 1941.

When Ned died in Newcastle General Hospital of kidney failure in 1943, Wilf, who had been missing in Malaya for 17 months, was known to be a Japanese prisoner of war.

Ned left £1,079 and one shilling, most of it in National Savings Certificates and Defence Bonds. But he didn't leave a will so a quarter of his estate went to the brother with whom he had fallen out. Alf, his barber brother got a share and rest trickled out in small streams to children of his two sisters.

My dad got £47-10s-8d.

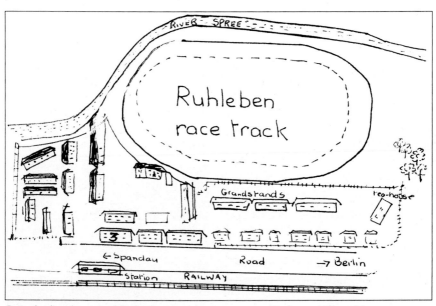

Rough sketch map of Ruhleben internment camp. Ned was billeted in barracks 3 near the road